CONCERT REPERTOIRE
VIOLIN
with piano

edited, selected and arranged by

Mary Cohen

FABER *ff* MUSIC

© 2006 by Faber Music Ltd
This edition first published in 2006 by Faber Music Ltd
Bloomsbury House 74–77 Great Russell Street London WC1B 3DA
Music processed by Jackie Leigh
Cover illustration by Drew Hillier
Cover design by Matthew Lee
Printed in England by Caligraving Ltd

ISBN10: 0-571-52440-0
EAN13: 978-0-571-52440-2

To buy Faber Music publications or to find out about the full range of titles available
please contact your local music retailer or Faber Music sales enquiries:

Faber Music Limited, Burnt Mill, Elizabeth Way, Harlow, CM20 2HX England
Tel: +44 (0)1279 82 89 82   Fax: +44 (0)1279 82 89 83
sales@fabermusic.com   fabermusic.com

CONTENTS

Corrente

from *Sonata in F Op.2 No.4, RV 20*

Antonio Vivaldi

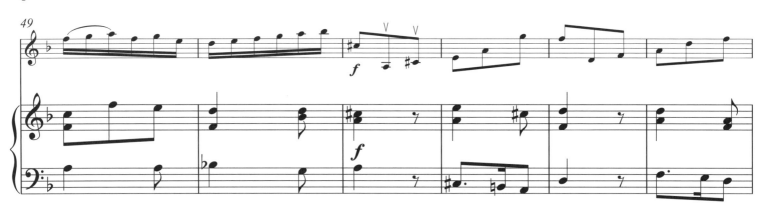

Without Care

8

Carl Reinecke

© 2006 by Faber Music Ltd.

Solveig's Song
from *Peer Gynt Suite*

Edvard Grieg

Serenade

Pyotr Ilyich Tchaikovsky

Air

from *Suite in D BWV 1068*

Johann Sebastian Bach

Sicilienne

Maria Teresia von Paradis

Torch Dance

from music to Shakespeare's *Henry VIII*

Edward German

Habanera

from *Carmen*

Georges Bizet

Allegretto quasi andantino ♩ = *c.*69

Hungarian Dance No.4

Johannes Brahms

Andante sostenuto ♩ = c.80

Chanson de matin

Op.15 No.2

Edward Elgar

Badinerie

from *Suite in B minor BWV 1067*

Johann Sebastian Bach

Allegro ♩ = 84

to Jenifer & David Matthews

Serenade

Peter Sculthorpe

VIOLIN MUSIC FROM FABER MUSIC

Fingerprints for Violin

EDITED BY MARY COHEN

A great collection of original, new music for players of Grade 1–4 standard. Each composer has tried to capture the essence of what makes them who they are and have left a musical 'fingerprint' for you to discover.

ISBN 0-571-52258-0

Real Repertoire for Violin

EDITED BY MARY COHEN

Essential repertoire for the intermediate violinist: a lasting inspiration to players everywhere.

ISBN 0-571-52155-X

Technique Takes Off!

MARY COHEN

Original, imaginative studies for solo violin covering a wide range of left and right-hand skills.

ISBN 0-571-51307-7

More Technique Takes Off!

MARY COHEN

Unaccompanied duets and studies, providing an imaginative and exciting course in developing vibrato, double-stopping and shifting.

ISBN 0-571-52484-2